REVIEW COPY
COURTESY OF
CAPSTONE PRESS

HORSES

The PERCHERON Horse

by Sarah Maass

Consultant:
Alex T. Christian
Executive Secretary
Percheron Horse Association of America
Fredericktown, Ohio

Capstone press

Mankato, Minnesota

Edge Books are published by Capstone Press,
151 Good Counsel Drive, P.O. Box 669, Mankato, Minnesota 56002.
www.capstonepress.com

Library of Congress Cataloging-in-Publication Data
Maass, Sarah.
    The Percheron horse / by Sarah Maass.
    p. cm.—(Edge Books. Horses)
    Summary: "Describes the Percheron draft horse, including its history,
physical features, and uses today"—Provided by publisher.
    Includes bibliographical references and index.
    ISBN-13: 978-0-7368-5460-3 (hardcover)
    ISBN-10: 0-7368-5460-6 (hardcover)
    1. Percheron horse—Juvenile literature. I. Title. II. Series.
SF293.P4M33 2006
636.1'5—dc22   2005017573

Editorial Credits
Carrie A. Braulick, editor; Juliette Peters, set designer; Bobbi J. Dey, book
    designer; Deirdre Barton, photo researcher/photo editor

Photo Credits
Bob Langrish, 11, 13, 14, 21, 27
Capstone Press/Gary Sundermeyer (objects), 9; Karon Dubke, 20, 26
Cecil Darnell, 5, 6, 8, 23
Gloria Muscarella/Cheval Photography, cover
Jack Horner Communications Inc., 22
Mark J. Barrett, back cover, 16–17, 29
Pamela (Pauley) MacKenzie, Brookfield, Nova Scotia, 12, 19, 25

1 2 3 4 5 6 11 10 09 08 07 06

Table of Contents

FEATURES

Chapter 1

Warhorse to Workhorse

Long ago, Percherons charged into battle carrying European knights. These large, strong horses were some of the best warhorses. Not even the heavy armor worn by the knights stopped Percherons from doing their jobs.

Early Beginnings

Before the 700s, Percherons were bred in an area of northwestern France called Le Perche. Breeders there have been producing horses longer than almost any other people in the world. Over time, the horses bred in Le Perche became known as Percherons.

Learn about:
- ★ **French stagecoaches**
- ★ **Jean Le Blanc**
- ★ **A Percheron registry**

Percherons are one of the oldest horse breeds.

The strength of Percherons helps them pull carriages.

The exact ancestry of Percherons is unknown. The horse breeders in Le Perche kept few records. Some people believe modern Percherons have Arabian, Thoroughbred, and Spanish Horse ancestry.

Diligence Horses

Knights proudly rode Percherons into battle throughout much of the Middle Ages (400–1400). But after gunpowder was invented in the 1300s, Percherons had different jobs. Europeans began using guns in wars. They wanted smaller horses that could move quickly.

Percherons then began pulling stagecoaches through French cities. These large, heavy carriages were loaded with mail or passengers.

Horses that pulled stagecoaches were called diligence horses. Percherons were popular for this job because they could trot long distances without tiring. Sometimes, Percherons pulled stagecoaches 35 miles (56 kilometers) in one day.

The Le Pin Stud Farm

In 1715, the French government started a horse breeding farm at Le Pin in the Le Perche area. The farm produced horses for the French government. Some of the horses used for breeding were Percherons.

In 1823, a Percheron stallion named Jean Le Blanc was born at the Le Pin stud farm. All of today's Percherons are descendants of this horse.

A few farmers still use Percherons for farmwork.

The Spread of Percherons

During the early 1800s, French cities were bursting at the seams. The overcrowding created a need for more carriage horses. Farmers also needed strong horses to pull farm equipment.

Percheron breeders quickly responded by producing horses with slightly larger builds. These Percherons were perfect for both jobs.

The Percheron's pulling power soon attracted fans in other parts of the world. In 1839, Edward Harris of New Jersey brought the first Percherons to the United States. Percherons quickly became the most popular draft horses in the country. People used Percherons and other draft horses for farmwork and to pull heavy loads.

In 1876, a group of Percheron breeders formed the Norman-Percheron Association. Percheron owners registered their horses' breeding records with the group. This registry is now known as the Percheron Horse Association of America. The association registers about 2,500 horses each year. It has registered nearly 300,000 Percherons since it began.

Chapter 2

Power and Grace

People usually hear a group of Percherons coming before they see them. The sound of the horses' hooves stomping on a street is hard to ignore. When the horses do come into view, they impress people with their strength and grace.

Size

A person who sees a Percheron for the first time is often amazed by its size. Horses are measured in hands. Each hand equals 4 inches (10 centimeters). Most adult Percherons stand between 16.2 and 17.3 hands tall at the withers, or top of the shoulders.

Learn about:
- ★ Size and weight
- ★ Colors
- ★ Personality

Percherons have sturdy builds with wide chests and thick legs.

Some are as tall as 19 hands. A Percheron's neck and head tower above an average-sized adult person.

Large dark eyes seem to show the Percheron's pleasant personality.

Appearance

Percherons have powerful builds. They have wide, muscular chests and necks. Percherons have especially strong hindquarters. Thick legs and large hooves support their heavy frames.

The Percheron's muscular build gives it a heavy weight. The horses usually weigh 1,600 to 2,400 pounds (730 to 1,100 kilograms), or about the weight of a small car.

Although Percherons are large, many people think they are the most graceful draft horses. Long, sloping shoulders give Percherons a high-stepping trot with a long stride.

A refined, delicately shaped head and large dark eyes add to the Percheron's elegance. Percherons carry their heads high, making them look proud.

A long stride sets Percherons apart from many other draft horses.

A calm, gentle personality makes Percherons
easy to handle.

Most Percherons are gray or black. A few are sorrel, bay, or roan. Sorrel is a red-brown color. Bay horses are red-brown with black manes, tails, and lower legs. Roan horses have dark coats with a mixture of white hairs. A few Percherons have white markings on their faces or legs.

Calm and Cooperative

The large size of Percherons makes some people uneasy around them. But there is no need to worry. Percherons are calm and gentle. They are often used in parades because they stay calm around crowds. Percherons also are cooperative and intelligent. They keep their willing attitudes even after many hours of hard work.

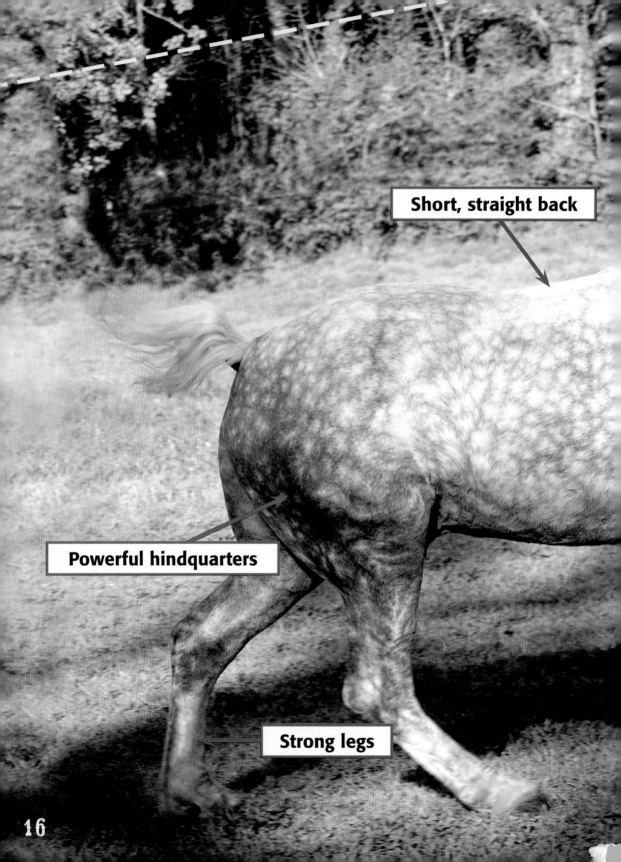

Short, straight back

Powerful hindquarters

Strong legs

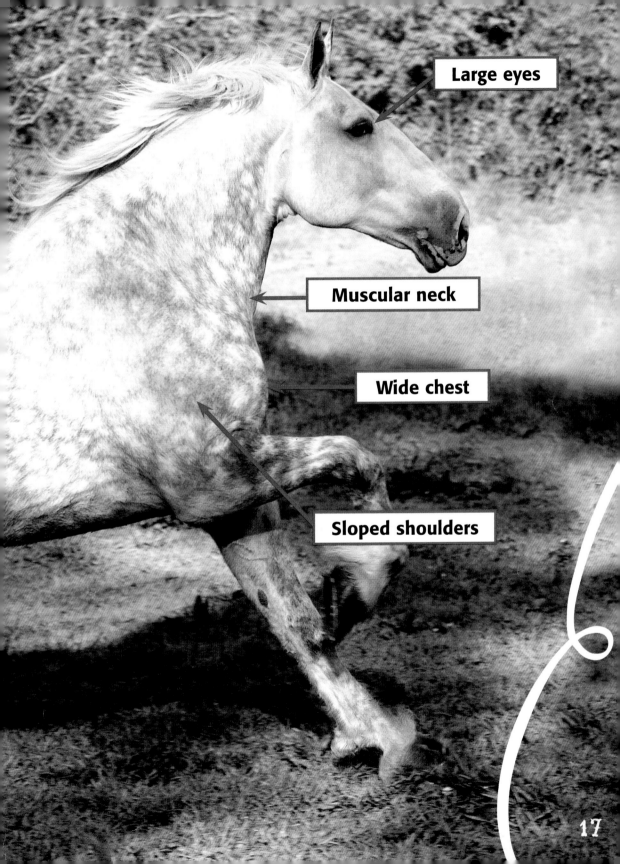

Large eyes

Muscular neck

Wide chest

Sloped shoulders

Chapter 3

Percherons in Harness

Percherons and pulling seem to go hand in hand. Many Percherons work as harness horses.

Training

Two-year-old Percherons are usually old enough to begin training. First, the horse becomes used to wearing a harness and a bridle. The harness is a set of straps that connect the horse to a vehicle. The bridle holds a metal piece, or bit, in the horse's mouth.

Long straps called lines attach to the bit. At first, the trainer walks behind the horse while holding the lines. This practice is called ground driving or long-lining.

Learn about:
★ Six-Horse Hitch Classic Series
★ Percherons in Disneyland
★ Heinz Percheron hitch

Trainers ground drive young Percherons before attaching the horses to a cart.

Later, the young horse is hitched to a lightweight cart. Trainers often hitch a young horse with an older, more experienced harness horse.

Hitches

Two or more horses harnessed together make up a hitch. Most hitches include two, four, or six horses. Two horses hitched together are called a team. Unicorn hitches include three horses. In these hitches, one horse leads the other two.

Six-horse hitches are common at horse shows. A six-horse hitch of Percherons trotting into an arena sounds like thunder. The ground shakes as the horses step high in perfect time with each other.

Each year, some of the best six-horse hitches compete in the North American Six-Horse Hitch Classic Series. Percheron, Belgian, Shire, and Clydesdale horses compete in the series.

The leading horse in a unicorn hitch must have especially good manners.

The Heinz Percheron hitch makes many public appearances.

Percherons in the Spotlight

Many Percherons pull carriages for weddings or other events. At Disneyland in Anaheim, California, Percheron and Belgian horses pull carriages called trolleys. The horses stay relaxed even with the noise and action of the busy amusement park.

Percherons are especially stylish parade horses. One famous eight-horse hitch of Percherons pulls a wagon for the H. J. Heinz Company. These horses appear in parades and festivals throughout North America.

Windermere Farms

Abe and Gerald Allebach have many reasons to be proud of their horses. They own Windermere Farms in Spring Mills, Pennsylvania. Percherons raised there have won more national and international titles than horses from any other Percheron farm. One of the farm's stallions, Black Home Duke, was the Premier Sire of North America 10 years in a row. This title is based on how often a stallion's offspring have won at major shows.

Chapter 4

Percherons in Action

There is a Percheron for almost any horse-related activity. Many Percherons are reliable riding horses. A few Percherons still work on farms. Some Percherons pull logs from forests. Percherons do less damage to forest floors than logging machinery does.

World Percheron Congress

Percherons show off their many uses at the World Percheron Congress. This show is held every three years in the United States, Canada, or France. People ride Percherons in Western and English pleasure classes. In the plowing class, horses are judged on the neatness and straightness of the plow's path, or furrow.

Learn about:
★ Pulling competitions
★ Caring for Percherons
★ Sport horses

Percherons in the logging industry pull heavy logs from forests.

Pulling Competitions

Some of the strongest Percherons compete in pulling competitions. In these events, a team pulls a sled loaded with weights. The horses try to pull the sled a certain distance. If the team succeeds, more weight is added to the sled. The team that pulls the heaviest load wins. At the 2004 World Percheron Congress, the winning team in the heavyweight pulling championship pulled 9,480 pounds (4,300 kilograms).

Owning a Percheron

Percheron owners must spend time and money on their horses. Like all horses, Percherons need regular hoof and veterinary care. Percheron owners should make sure their horses have stalls and exercise areas with plenty of room. Percherons eat and drink more than smaller horses like Arabians and Quarter Horses.

Percherons are big horses with big hearts. Their pleasant personalities and many uses make them one of North America's best-loved draft horses.

Producing Sport Horses

Some horse breeders mate Percherons with Thoroughbreds, Andalusians, and other breeds. The strong, athletic horses they produce are making their mark in the sport horse world. Sport horses are mainly used for jumping and dressage. In dressage, a horse and rider complete a pattern of advanced moves.

Some talented sport horses are foals of the Percheron stallion Cottonwood Flame. Cottonwood Flame competed in Grand Prix, the highest level of dressage.

Fast Facts:
The Percheron Horse

Name: Percherons receive their name from the area of Le Perche in northwestern France. Percherons were first bred there.

History: The exact ancestry of Percherons is unknown. Percherons were used as warhorses in the Middle Ages. Later, they pulled stagecoaches in France. The first Percherons arrived in the United States in 1839.

Height: Most Percherons are between 16.2 and 17.3 hands (about 5.5 feet or 1.7 meters) tall at the withers. Each hand equals 4 inches (10 centimeters).

Weight: 1,600 to 2,400 pounds (730 to 1,100 kilograms)

Colors: Most Percherons are black or gray, but some are roan, bay, or sorrel.

Features: muscular hindquarters; strong legs; wide, deep chest; short, straight back; sloped shoulders; refined head; large eyes

Personality: gentle, intelligent, calm, cooperative

Abilities: Percherons are mainly used as harness horses. Some people ride Percherons.

Life span: Most Percherons live about 15 to 20 years. Some live 30 years or more.

Glossary

armor (AR-mur)—metal covering worn by knights to protect them in battle

bridle (BRYE-duhl)—the straps that fit around a horse's head and connect to a bit to control a horse while riding or driving

dressage (druh-SAHJ)—a riding style in which horses complete a pattern while doing advanced moves

foal (FOHL)—a horse that is less than 1 year old

furrow (FUR-oh)—the groove cut by a plow when it turns over the soil

harness (HAR-niss)—a set of leather straps and metal pieces that connect a horse to a carriage, plow, wagon, or other vehicle

registry (REH-juh-stree)—an organization that keeps track of the ancestry for horses of one breed

stagecoach (STAYJ-kohch)—a large vehicle used in the past to carry passengers and mail over long distances

stallion (STAL-yuhn)—an adult male horse that can be used for breeding

Read More

Dalgleish, Sharon. *Working Horses.* Farm Animals. Philadelphia: Chelsea Clubhouse, 2005.

Hull, Mary E. *The Horse in Harness.* The Horse Library. Philadelphia: Chelsea House, 2002.

Ransford, Sandy. *The Kingfisher Illustrated Horse and Pony Encyclopedia.* Boston: Kingfisher, 2004.

Internet Sites

FactHound offers a safe, fun way to find Internet sites related to this book. All of the sites on FactHound have been researched by our staff.

Here's how:

1. Visit *www.facthound.com*
2. Type in this special code **0736854606** for age-appropriate sites. Or enter a search word related to this book for a more general search.
3. Click on the **Fetch It** button.

FactHound will fetch the best sites for you!

Index